Grandpa the birdman

Nelson

Trog was sitting by the tree.

'What's the matter?' asked Mother,
'aren't you well today?'

'I'm fed up,' said Trog.
'I don't know what to do with myself.'

'You could help me,' said Mother.

'I helped you yesterday,' said Trog,
'and I helped Father the day before.'

'I've got an idea,' Grandpa said.
'I know what you can do.
You can watch me play at birds!'

'Birds?' said Trog,
'How do you play at birds?
Birds can fly.'

'I know,' said Grandpa,
'that's the idea.
When I was a boy like you
I was the best birdman
you have ever seen.'

'That sounds like a good game,'
Trog said.

'Show me how to play.'

'Come on then,' said Grandpa.

'I will scrape some deerskins
with a knife
until they are very thin and light.
You can find some long thin branches
and creepers.'

'I will tie the skins to the branches
and make a pair of wings.

I hold the wings in the air
and run downhill.
If I am as good as I used to be,
I shall fly.
You just watch.'

Grandpa scraped away at the skins
and Trog found some long thin branches
and creepers.

Grandpa tied the branches together
and put on the skins.

'There,' he said.
'What a good pair of wings!
Come on, Trog,
let's go to the top of the steep hill
by the river.'

'I can't wait to see this,' said Trog.

HOORAY!
go to it Grandpa!!

They went to the top of the hill.

'Now watch the best birdman in the land,'
said Grandpa.

He held the wings above his head
and started to run down
the steep side of the hill.

He made little jumps as he ran,
and the wings lifted him
up off the ground.

'Well, I flew a little bit,
didn't I?' said Grandpa.

'Can I have a go now?' said Trog.

'All right,' said Grandpa,
'but I don't think you will be able
to fly like I did.'

Trog held the wings and ran down the hill
as fast as he could.

Halfway down the hill he gave a big jump.
The wings lifted him up
and carried him nearly to the bottom.

'This is great!'
he shouted up to Grandpa.

'I'm going to have another go,'
Trog said,
when he reached the top again.

'I think I shall be
just as good a birdman as you.'

Grandpa just looked at him
and didn't say a word.

'We'll see about that,'
said Grandpa to himself.

The next morning
Trog was dying to play birdmen again
but Grandpa said no.

'Those wings were just right for you,'
he told Trog,
'but I am so much bigger than you
I must make a bigger pair for myself.
As soon as I have made them
we will go flying again.'

18

When the new wings were made,
the two of them went
to the top of the hill again.

Mother and Father
came to watch the new game.

The wind was very strong.

Trog went down the hill first.
He had only gone a little way
when his wings lifted him up and he flew
right to the bottom of the hill.

'Well done!' shouted Mother and Father.

'Now beat **that** if you can, Grandpa,'
said Trog,
when he had climbed
to the top of the hill again.

Grandpa said nothing.
He carefully lifted up
his giant pair of wings
and looked down the hill.
Then he set off.

'Be careful!' shouted Mother.
'Do be careful!'

The wind was blowing a gale.

Grandpa ran as fast as he could
and gave a big jump.
To his surprise he flew up in the air
like a rocket.

One minute he was the right way up
and the next minute he was upside down
and still going higher.

'My goodness!' he yelled.
'What shall I do now?'

He went higher and higher.
Trog, Mother and Father
couldn't believe their eyes.

'He'll break his leg
when he lands,' said Mother.

'Or both his legs,' said Father.

'Or his legs and his arms,' said Trog.
'I've never seen anything like it.
He's nearly out of sight.
He's a real birdman, isn't he?'

Grandpa was whizzing along,
first this way up, then that way up.
He was so frightened
he closed his eyes tight
and just hoped for the best.

He went so fast that he was soon over the land of the Quickerwits.

'Look at that bird!' shouted the chief
to the rest of the tribe.

'Quick! Shoot it down.
It's so big, it will feed us for days.'

They ran for their bows and arrows
and Grandpa opened his eyes
to see sharp arrows whizzing past him.

Don't Shoot

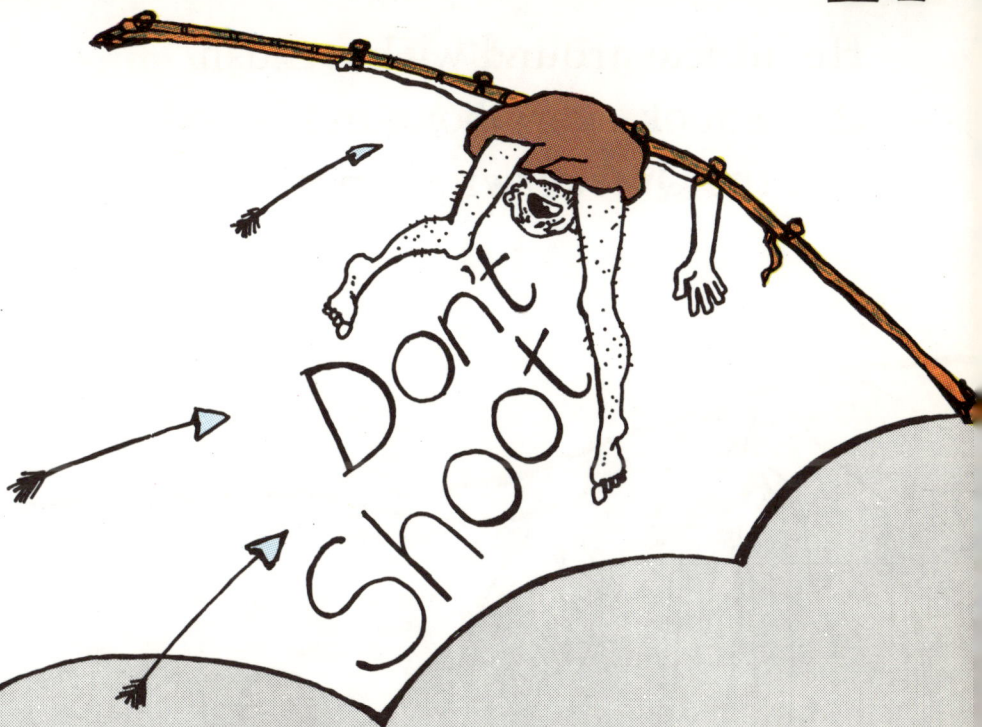

'Don't shoot!' he yelled.
'Don't shoot! It's me—Grandpa Gripe.'

'Stop!' shouted the chief.
'I know that voice. It's Grandpa.'

The tribe put down their bows
and luckily for Grandpa
the wind began to drop.
He came slowly to the ground.

He hit the ground with a crash
that shook every bone in his body,
and the Quickerwits ran up to him.

'Are you all right?' they asked.

'I'm fine now I'm on the ground,'
said Grandpa.
'It's better than being up in the air.'

'Have a rest,' they said,
'and then we'll take you home.'

Mother had never expected
to see him alive again.
Trog and Father ran up to him.
'My goodness,' Trog said to Grandpa.
'That was the best game
you have ever played.'

'I know,' replied Grandpa,
'but you can play it by yourself
from now on.
Flying is for real birds
and not for me.'